Sprout™
GROWING WITH GOD

BIBLE

WRITTEN & ILLUSTRATED
BY THE DE VILLIERS FAMILY

WATERBROOK
PRESS

SPROUT BIBLE
PUBLISHED BY WATERBROOK PRESS
12265 Oracle Boulevard, Suite 200
Colorado Springs, Colorado 80921
A division of Random House, Inc.

Unless otherwise indicated, all stories are adapted from Scripture as found in the *Holy Bible, New International Version*®. NIV®. Copyright © 1973, 1978, 1984 by International Bible Society. Used by permission of Zondervan Publishing House. All rights reserved.

ISBN 1-4000-7194-1

Copyright © 2006 by The de Villiers Family

Published in association with the literary agency of Alive Communications, Inc., 7680 Goddard Street, Suite 200, Colorado Springs, CO 80920.

Library of Congress Cataloging-in-Publication Data

Sprout Bible : thirty-four favorite Bible stories for kids / written and illustrated by the de Villiers family.— 1st ed.
    p. cm. — (Learn and grow with Sprout)
  ISBN 1-4000-7194-1
  1. Bible stories, English.   I. Series.
BS551.3.S67 2005
220.9'505—dc22
                                    2005027282

Printed in China
2006—First Edition

10 9 8 7 6 5 4 3 2 1

TABLE OF CONTENTS

The Old Testament

Creation - PAGE 9

Noah's Ark - PAGE 15

God's Promise to Abraham - PAGE 21

Jacob and Esau - PAGE 27

Joseph's Coat of Many Colors - PAGE 33

Baby Moses in a Basket - PAGE 39

Moses Parts the Water - PAGE 45

The Ten Commandments - PAGE 51

The Walls of Jericho - PAGE 57

Samuel Hears a Voice - PAGE 63

David and Goliath - PAGE 69

King Solomon - PAGE 75

God Brings Elijah Food - PAGE 81

Queen Esther - PAGE 87

The Blazing Furnace - PAGE 93

Daniel in the Lions' Den - PAGE 99

Jonah and the Fish - PAGE 105

The New Testament

Mary, Jesus's Mother - PAGE 111

The Birth of Jesus - PAGE 115

The Wise Men - PAGE 121

John the Baptist - PAGE 127

The Paralyzed Man - PAGE 133

Jesus's Disciples - PAGE 139

Jesus Teaches the People - PAGE 145

Jesus Calms the Storm - PAGE 149

Jesus and the Children - PAGE 153

Loaves and Fishes - PAGE 157

Jesus Meets Zacchaeus - PAGE 163

Jesus and the Cross - PAGE 169

Easter Morning - PAGE 175

Jesus's Gift to His Followers - PAGE 181

The Road to Damascus - PAGE 187

Paul and Silas in Jail - PAGE 193

John Tells of Jesus's Return - PAGE 199

Creation
Genesis 1-2

In the very beginning, long before the world was made, God was there.

He decided to create something wonderful. First, He made the heavens and the earth. Everything was dark and covered with water, so God said, "Let there be light"—and, whoosh, a bright light shone all around! God was happy with the light. He separated the light from the darkness and called it day; the darkness He called night. This was the very first day.

On the second day, He made a large space above the water and called this the sky.

Sprout says:
Have you ever wondered where stars come from?

On the third day, God gathered together all the water and called it the seas. He called the dry ground the land. God made many different kinds of plants and trees to grow on the land. They produced delicious fruit and seeds. God saw all the things He had made, and He was happy.

On the fourth day, God made two big lights in the sky, the golden sun to shine during the day and the silvery moon to shine at night. He also made the sparkling stars and placed them in the night sky. These signs show the seasons, days, and years.

Did you know that
the stripes on each
zebra are different,
and that God made
each person his or
her own fingerprint
pattern?

On the fifth day, God made all the creatures
that live in the sea: small and big fish, dolphins,
crabs, and turtles. He also made bright, beauti-
fully colored birds to fly in the sky.

On the sixth day, God made all the creatures
that live on the land. Some were tall like giraffes
and some were as small like mice, but each was
special. On the same day, He made the first
man and woman. He placed them on earth
to take care of the fish in the sea and the birds

in the sky and all the animals that lived on the earth. He also told them to eat the seeds and fruits from plants and trees.

God was very happy with everything that He had made.

On the seventh day, God was finished making the world and everything in it, so He rested from all His work. God called this day holy because it was the day that He rested.

Growth Spurt

- Do you think you can count all the stars in the sky?
- Do you know how many fish there are in the sea?
- Do you know how many hairs are on your head?

God knows how many stars are in the sky because He placed them there. He also knows how many fish are in the sea. He even knows how many hairs are on your head because He made YOU!

Noah's Ark
Genesis 6-9

When God saw how wicked the people who lived on earth had become, it made Him very sad. He was sorry that He had created them and decided to destroy the earth and all the people, animals, and birds that lived on it.

Noah was the only person who pleased Him. So God said to Noah, "I am going to destroy the whole earth and everything on it. I want you to build a big boat from cypress wood and cover it inside and out with tar to make it waterproof." God told Noah how to make the boat. It had to be 450 feet long, 75 feet wide, and 45 feet high, with a roof and a door. When it was finished, God instructed Noah to take his whole family onto the ark along with animals of every kind.

He also had to take enough food to feed them all. Noah did everything that God told him to do. He was 600 years old.

When they were all safely inside, it started to rain, and it did not stop for forty days and forty nights. The water covered the whole earth. Even the highest mountains were under water. All the living things on the earth were destroyed, but Noah, his family, and the animals were safe inside the ark. The floodwaters covered the earth for 150 days. Then God sent a wind to slowly dry up the water. The ark landed on top of Mount Ararat.

Noah sent out a dove, but it came back because it could find nowhere to perch. Noah knew the earth was still covered with water. Noah waited for seven days and sent the dove out again.

Did you know that the ark was nearly as long as a football field and the width was half as wide as a football field?

This time it returned with a freshly picked olive leaf in its beak. After seven more days, he once again let the dove out, but this time it did not come back. So Noah opened the door of the ark and saw that the earth was completely dry. Then he and his family and all the animals left the ark.

God was pleased and said to Noah, "I have set my rainbow in the clouds. It will remind you of my promise to you that I will never again destroy the earth by floodwater."

Growth Spurt

- Have you ever seen a rainbow in the sky?
- What does a rainbow remind us of?
- Do you think that God loves you?

God put a rainbow in the sky
to remind us that He loves us
and will always care for us!

God's Promise to Abraham

Genesis 12-18, 21

"It's time for you to move," God said to a 75-year-old man who lived in Haran. The man's name was Abram. "I'll show you a new place to live," God promised. So Abram packed up everything he owned. He took his wife, Sarai; his nephew, Lot; and all of their animals and shepherds and set out for Canaan.

When they arrived there, God appeared to Abram and said to him, "I will give this whole land to your children." As time passed, Abram and Lot became very rich men.

Sprout says:
Have you ever made a promise?

They owned many sheep and cattle and lots
of gold and silver, but their shepherds were
constantly fighting. So Abram went to Lot and
said, "We are family. Let's not fight anymore.
You choose the place where you want to live."
Lot picked the best land, on the plain of Jordan,
and Abram went to live in Canaan.

Many years went by, and Abram did not have
any children. He went to God and said, "What
good is it if I am rich but have no children to
inherit everything I own?" Then God took him

outside and said, "Look up at the sky and count the stars if you can. That's how big your family will be." Abram believed what God told him, and this pleased God very much.

Abram was 99 years old when God came to him once again and said, "I am here to remind you that I am going to give you a huge family. I am changing your name to Abraham, which means father of fathers. I am changing your wife's name to Sarah, and she will have a son. Your children and grandchildren and great-grandchildren will become a great nation, and I will be their God. This is my promise to you."

Abraham was so overwhelmed that he fell flat on his face, laughing.

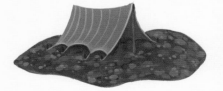

Did you know that the tents were usually made with cloth spun from goat hair?

Some time later, Abraham saw three men standing near his tent. He asked them to come in and have something to eat. While Sarah was preparing the food, she overheard the visitors telling Abraham that she would soon have a baby son. This made her laugh, and she thought to herself, *"I am way too old to have a baby."*

God said to Abraham, "Tell Sarah that nothing is impossible for God, and by next year she will have a son. You will name him Isaac (which means

'laughter'), and I will keep my promise to you and all of your family forever and ever."

Abraham was 100 years old when Isaac was born, and he threw a big party.

- Is it easy to keep a promise?
- Do you think God always keeps His promises?

God kept His promise by giving Isaac to Abraham and Sarah. He always keeps His promises to us!

Jacob and Esau
Genesis 25, 27

Abraham's grandchildren were twins. Esau was born first, and he loved hunting. Jacob was born second, and he preferred to stay at home. When their father, Isaac, was old, and he could no longer see very well, he called Esau, his favorite son. "Go and catch some game and cook a tasty meal for me," he said. "Then I will give you my blessing before I die."

Their mother, Rebekah, overheard them. As soon as Esau left to go hunting, she ran to Jacob and said, "Quickly go and fetch two young goats and bring them to me so that I can prepare a great meal

Sprout says:
Have you ever played a trick on someone?

for your father. Then he will give his blessing to you instead of Esau." She did this because she loved Jacob more than Esau.

Jacob went to fetch the goats and brought them to his mother. She cooked a tasty meal just the way Isaac liked it. Then she took the skins from the goats and wrapped them around Jacob's arms so they would feel hairy like Esau's. She also put some of his brother's clothes on him. Rebekah told Jacob to take the food she had prepared to his father and ask for his blessing.

Jacob went to his father and said, "My father, here is the meal you asked for. Sit up and eat, and then give me your blessing."

Did you know that goats provide milk, butter, cheese, and meat? Goat skin was used to make containers for water and wine.

Isaac said to Jacob, "Come a little closer so that I can feel your arms. Your voice sounds like Jacob, but your arms feel hairy. Are you really my son Esau?"

"Yes I am," answered Jacob.

Then Isaac sat up and ate some of the food. When he was finished, he said to Jacob, "Come here and give me a kiss." Isaac smelled Esau's scent from the clothes that Jacob wore, so he thought it was Esau and gave him his blessing.

Jacob had just left his father's tent when Esau came back from hunting. He cooked a meal from the game he caught and took it to his father saying, "I have prepared a tasty meal for you, father. Come and eat, and then give me your blessing."

Isaac sat up and asked him, "Who are you?"

"I am your firstborn son," replied Esau.

Isaac began to tremble and said, "Your brother Jacob has tricked us. He brought me food, and I gave him my blessing." Esau was very upset and begged his father to bless him also. Isaac said, "I will bless you, but you will always serve your brother."

This made Esau very angry, and he decided to kill Jacob after his father's death. When Rebekah heard about this, she helped Jacob move away to live with her brother Laban, so that he would be safe.

Growth Spurt

- Has anyone ever tricked you?
- How did you feel when you realized that you had been tricked?

Jacob lied to his father, so he had to run away from home. God is unhappy when we lie.

Joseph's Coat of Many Colors
Genesis 37-47

Jacob loved his son Joseph more than his other sons. One day Joseph's father gave him a beautiful coat made from brightly colored fabrics. When his eleven brothers saw the coat, they became very jealous because they realized how much more their father loved Joseph. They were so mad that they did not even want to speak to him.

Then Joseph dreamed that his brothers were like sheaves of grain bowing down to him. This made them very angry. "You think that you are going to rule over us," they said, and they hated him even more.

Sprout says:
Have you ever wanted something that wasn't yours?

One day his father called Joseph and said,
"Please go out to the fields where your brothers
are looking after the sheep. I want you to see how
they are doing and then hurry home to tell me."
So Joseph went off to find them.

When his brothers saw him coming in the
distance, they began making plans to kill him.
His oldest brother, Reuben, stopped them and
said, "Why don't we throw him in this dry well
instead?" Reuben was secretly planning to rescue
Joseph later and take him back to his father.

As soon as Joseph reached his brothers, they took off his beautiful colored coat and threw him into the empty well. Then they sat down and ate a meal together.

While they were eating, some traders came along who were on their way to Egypt to sell spices, ointments, and perfumes. Reuben was away, but Judah, another brother of Joseph's, said, "Why don't we sell Joseph to these traders, and they will take him to Egypt?" They all agreed that it was a good plan. So they lifted Joseph from the well and sold him to the traders for twenty shekels of silver.

When Reuben returned, he saw that Joseph was not in the well anymore. "What am I going to do?" he cried. "What can I tell our father?"

The brothers took Joseph's colorful coat and showed it to their father and pretended not to know what had happened to him. Jacob cried and tore his clothes because he thought that Joseph was dead. He was very sad.

In the meantime, the traders took Joseph to Egypt and sold him as a slave. God blessed everything that Joseph did. He became a mighty man who eventually saved the whole country, including his own brothers.

The traders used camels to cross the desert because they could go for several days without water and carry over 400 pounds!

Growth Spurt

- Have you ever been jealous of someone?
- Has anyone ever been jealous of you?
- How does God feel when you act jealously?

Even though Joseph's brothers were jealous and mean, God took care of him in everything that he did.

Baby Moses in a Basket
Exodus 1-2

They were big. They were mighty. And the king of Egypt was scared. He thought this large nation living in his land would go against him in war. Who were they? They were the children and grandchildren and great-grandchildren of Abraham, Isaac, and Jacob.

The king, called Pharaoh, decided to make life difficult for the Israelites. He made them work very hard, making bricks and mortar to

Sprout says:
Have you ever found something really fun?

build big cities. But the harder they worked, the more their families grew. They had many children. Pharaoh was not pleased. He ordered that all the baby boys must be thrown into the Nile River.

One Israelite woman had a baby boy. When she saw how special he was, she tried to hide him. After three months she could no longer keep him hidden. So she took a basket made of papyrus and covered it with tar to make it waterproof.

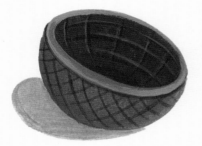

The Egyptians used reeds from the Nile River to weave baskets. These baskets were often used to carry grain during the harvesting time.

Then she put her son into the basket and floated it among the reeds at the edge of the river. The baby's older sister watched to see what would happen to him.

Soon afterward, Pharaoh's daughter came to bathe in the Nile. As she was walking along with her handmaids, she spotted the little basket among the reeds. She asked one of the servants to fetch it and was very surprised to see a baby boy. He was crying, and she felt sorry for him.

"This must be one of the Israelite babies," she said. Then the baby's sister came over and asked, "Would you like me to go and get someone to take care of him for you?"

"Yes, go quickly," replied Pharaoh's daughter. So the sister went and fetched the baby's mother, who nursed him until he was older. Then she took him back to Pharaoh's daughter, and he became her son. She named him Moses, which means "pulled-out," because she'd pulled him from the water.

Moses lived in Pharaoh's palace and grew up strong.

- Have you ever hidden something?
- Why did Moses's mother hide him?
- Was God happy when Pharaoh's daughter found Moses?

Moses's mother saved him by hiding him in the basket. It was all part of God's special plan to make Moses a great leader.

Moses Parts the Water

Exodus 3-14

Fire! Moses saw a burning bush, but it wasn't burning up. He went closer to see this strange sight, and the voice of God spoke to him. God said, "My people are suffering. I am sending you to Pharaoh. Tell him to let the Israelites leave Egypt."

Moses was afraid and asked, "How will I know what to say?"

God told him not to worry and said, "I will be with you and give you the right words."

Sprout says:
Have you ever needed help to do something?

45

So Moses went to Pharaoh and said, "The Lord God says: 'Let my people go to the desert so they can hold a festival for me.'"

But Pharaoh replied, "Why should I listen to this God?" and he made them work even harder.

Then God sent ten plagues on Egypt—blood, frogs, lice, flies, disease, boils, hail, locusts, darkness, and finally death. Pharaoh gave up. "Go. Hurry up and take all your things and leave," he ordered.

So the Israelites quickly grabbed everything and fled into the desert. God showed them where to go with a pillar of cloud during the day and a pillar of fire at night. When they came to the Red Sea, they stopped to camp.

Meanwhile, Pharaoh changed his mind and wanted the Israelites to return to Egypt. He sent his army to bring them back. The Israelites were terrified when they saw the chariots, horsemen, and troops chasing them. "Why did you bring us out into the desert to die?" they asked Moses.

"Wait and see how God will save you today," replied Moses. Then Moses stretched out his hand over the sea, and the water divided in two. The Israelites walked right through on dry ground to the other side. When Pharaoh's army

chased after the Israelites across the sea, Moses
raised his hand again. The water washed away
all the Egyptian chariots, horsemen, and soldiers.

"Hurrah!" the Israelites cheered.
"God has saved us from Pharaoh's army!"

To celebrate they sang songs and praised God.

Growth Spurt

- Have you ever helped someone?
- Has anyone ever helped you?
- How did God help the Israelites?

God sent Moses to help
the Israelites escape from
Pharaoh. He will always
help you, too!

The Ten Commandments
Exodus 19-20

Flashes of lightening! Claps of thunder and ear-piercing trumpet blasts! What was going on at the top of Mount Sinai? The Israelites were terrified. It had been only three months since they'd escaped from Egypt and set up camp at the foot of the mountain. And now this!

Moses had heard God calling, so he went up to the top of the mountain to meet with Him. God said to him, "Remind the people how I saved them from the Egyptians and brought them safely to this place. Then ask them if they

Sprout says:
Do you always follow the rules?

51

are ready to obey me in everything, so that they can become my most treasured nation on earth." Moses went back to the Israelites and gave them God's message. They all answered, "We will do everything that God wants."

Three days later a thick cloud came down over the mountain. Moses led the people out to meet God at the bottom of the mountain. It was covered in thick smoke and fire because God was there. The whole mountain was shaking violently, and the trumpet blasts grew louder and louder. Then God

spoke to Moses, "Tell the people not to come any closer, but you come up here to me."
So Moses went up into the dark cloud.

This is what God said to him:

1. I am your God, and you cannot have any other gods.
2. You must not make any idols to worship.
3. You must not use my name as a curse word.
4. You can work for six days, but the seventh day is holy and you must rest.
5. You must always respect and obey your father and mother.
6. You must not kill anyone.
7. You must not love someone else's husband or wife.
8. You must not steal.
9. You must not tell lies.
10. You must not want something that belongs to someone else.

After God was finished speaking to Moses,
He gave him two stone tablets with the words
of the Ten Commandments on them. God had
written the words with His own hand.

Then Moses told the people everything that
God had said—all of God's rules. They agreed
to obey them all. Moses built an altar and
worshiped God.

- Why do we have rules?
- Is it hard to always follow the rules?
- Does God want us to follow His rules?

God gave us the Ten Commandments, so that we would know how He wants us to live. He is happy when we obey His rules.

The Walls of Jericho
Joshua

Be strong and courageous!" That's what God told Joshua after Moses died. Joshua was the new leader of the Israelites. God spoke to him and said, "Lead the people across the Jordan River." So Joshua told the people to pack their belongings and get ready to cross the Jordan River into a new land.

Joshua sent two spies into the land to check out the city of Jericho. When they arrived at the city, they went to stay at the home of Rahab. Soon the king of Jericho heard about the spies and sent his soldiers to capture them.

Sprout says:
Do you like to
be the leader?

But Rahab hid them on the roof of her house. The spies were thankful that she had saved their lives, and they promised to save her family when the Israelites attacked Jericho. They told her to tie a scarlet cord in the window, so that they would know which house was hers. Then she lowered them down out of the window with a rope, so that they could escape.

The ark of the covenant was made out of expensive acacia wood and covered with pure gold and held the Ten Commandments.

Early in the morning, Joshua and the Israelites set out. They stopped at the Jordan River and camped. After three days Joshua spoke to them and said, "Today you will see what amazing things God can do. Get ready to follow the ark of the covenant."

As soon as the priests carrying the ark of the covenant stepped into the Jordan River, the water stopped flowing and their path was dry. The whole nation of Israel could walk through on dry ground to the land that God had promised to them.

By then the city of Jericho was locked up, and no one could go in or come out. But God gave Joshua

a plan, and Joshua and his people did as God commanded: Every day for six days they marched around the city, and on the seventh day they marched around seven times. Then the priests blew their trumpets, and the people let out a mighty roar. The walls of the city came tumbling down!

The Israelites went into Jericho and destroyed everything in it. They saved only Rahab and her family, as they had promised, and she went to live with them.

Growth Spurt

- What does a leader do?
- Who was the new leader of the Israelites?
- What happened when Joshua led the people to Jericho?

The Israelites followed Joshua to Jericho. He was a good leader because he told the people what God wanted them to do. So God helped them win the battle for Jericho. God is happy when you're a good leader!

Samuel Hears a Voice
1 Samuel 1-3

Elkanah had two wives, Hannah and Peninnah. Peninnah had children, but Hannah had none. This made Hannah very sad, and she longed to have a baby.

Every year they would go to the temple at Shiloh to make a sacrifice to God. While they were at the temple, Peninnah would taunt Hannah because she had no children. Hannah was heartsick.

Sprout says:
Do you always listen?

Every year the Israelites traveled to the shrine at Shiloh to celebrate the harvest and their covenant with God. This was called the Feast of Booths.

One year she begged God to give her a child. Hannah promised Him that if she had a son, she would give him up to become a priest in the temple. Eli, the priest, saw how upset she was and he said, "God will hear your prayers. Go in peace."

Soon Hannah had a son, and she named him Samuel. She cared for him until he was old enough to live in the temple. She said to Eli, "God has given me a son, and now I am bringing him to you so that he can serve God. This was what I promised to do." After this, God blessed Hannah, and she had five more children.

Samuel grew up strong and served God.
One night as Eli and Samuel were sleeping in
the temple, Samuel heard a voice calling him,
"Samuel, Samuel!" Thinking that it was Eli,
he went to the priest and said, "Here I am.
Did you call me?"

Eli replied, "Go back to bed. I did not call you."

Once again Samuel heard the voice calling him. When it happened a third time, Eli realized that it was God calling Samuel, so he told him, "Go and lie down and when you hear the voice, say, 'Speak God; I am listening.'"

God called again, "Samuel, Samuel!"

This time Samuel answered saying, "Speak God; I am listening." God told Samuel everything that He was going to do for Israel. From that day on, Samuel served God as a priest and a prophet.

Did you know that during the time of Samuel the children played lots of games like you do? Archeologists have found carvings of children playing leapfrog in Egypt.

- How does it feel when someone doesn't listen to you?
- Did Samuel listen to God?
- What did God tell Samuel?

Samuel listened when
God spoke to him.
So God made him the
most powerful prophet
in all of Israel.

David and Goliath
1 Samuel 16-17

What's so special about David? He was the youngest son of Jesse, and he looked after sheep. What made David special was that he was chosen by God to become king of Israel!

When David was still young, the Israelites were at war with the Philistines. The Philistine army was camped on one side of the valley, and the Israelite army was on the other side. Each day Goliath came out and stood in front of the Israelite army.

Sprout says:
Do you ever feel too small?

He was a huge giant—over nine feet tall—and he wore shiny bronze armor and carried a heavy spear. He shouted at them, "Send out your best man to fight against me. If he wins we will be your slaves, but if I win you will become our slaves."

Goliath did this every morning and every night for forty days. The Israelites were terrified and did not know what to do.

One day David was in the Israelite camp visiting his brothers when he heard Goliath shouting his usual challenge. He saw how frightened the Israelites were of him and said, "Who does he think he is to shout at the army of God? I will go and fight him!"

When King Saul heard this, he tried to stop David and said, "You are so young, and Goliath is a mighty soldier. You don't stand a chance against him."

But David replied, "When I was protecting my sheep, God helped me to kill lions and bears. He will also help me to kill this giant Philistine." So David went down to the river and picked up five smooth stones. He placed them in his bag, took his sling in his hand, and went out to meet Goliath.

The giant looked down at David scornfully. "Come on. Let's fight," he sneered.

The shepherd's sling was made by braiding wool twine. Ancient armies used them because they were cheap to make and portable.

"You have a sword and a spear, but I come in the name of God. He will help me win this fight," David said to Goliath. David put a stone into his sling and threw it at Goliath. The stone hit in him right in the middle of his forehead. The giant came crashing down to the ground, flat on his face. When the Philistines saw that their hero was dead, they turned around and ran away. The Israelites cheered and chased after them.

Growth Spurt

- How did God use David?
- Can God use you even though you're small?
- Do you want God to use you?

Even though David was small, God gave him courage and helped him defeat Goliath. God can use you, too!

King Solomon

1 Kings 3-8

Y ou can ask me for anything that you want, and I will give it to you." That's what God told Solomon one night in a dream. Solomon was the son of David and the new king of Israel. What would he choose?

Solomon answered, "Please give me a heart that listens to you, so that I will know right from

Sprout says:
Do you like to build things?

wrong and be able to rule wisely over the people of Israel." God was very pleased with his request and told him that he would become the wisest man of all time.

Under Solomon's rule Israel grew strong and there was peace in the land. So he decided that it was time to build a temple to honor God. He ordered cedar trees to be cut for timber, huge blocks of stone to be cut for the foundations, and thousands of men to come to work as builders. All the wood and stones were cut exactly to size, far away from the place where the temple was being built. No hammers or chisels were used at the temple site so that it was very quiet and respectful there.

The temple was a beautiful building. It had lovely carved wooden doors, walls made of

cedar wood, and gold covering the whole inside—
including the walls, the ceilings, and the floors.
It took Solomon seven years to build the temple.

When the building was completed, Solomon called on the leaders of the tribes of Israel to bring the ark of the covenant to the temple. The priests carried it into the temple and placed it in the inner sanctuary—the Holy Place. The glory of God filled the temple, and the whole building was filled with a cloud.

Solomon stood before the altar and prayed to God and thanked Him for keeping his promises.

Solomon's temple was built on a hill overlooking Jerusalem. Since it was meant to last forever, the walls were 10 feet thick. Although it stood for 400 years, none of it is left today.

Growth Spurt

- What kinds of things do you like to build?
- What did Solomon build for God?
- What did Solomon do once he'd finished building the temple?

Solomon honored God by building a beautiful temple for the people to worship in. God kept His promises and was very pleased.

God Brings Elijah Food
1 Kings 16-17

After Solomon died, Israel had many kings. Some were good and others were wicked, but the wickedest of all was King Ahab. He disobeyed God in everything and even built a temple so that the Israelites could worship the false god, Baal. He made God so angry—angrier than He had ever been with any other king.

Then God spoke to his prophet Elijah and said, "Go and tell the king that I will not send rain for the next few years. There will be a

Sprout says:
Have you ever needed something?

81

severe drought and not enough food for every-one. I want you to leave and go to Kerith and hide there."

Elijah did as God had told him, and he went and camped in Kerith next to a small stream. Every day God sent the ravens to bring food to him. They brought bread and meat, which he ate for breakfast and dinner. He drank fresh water from the stream.

Eventually the stream also dried up. God spoke to him again and said, "Go to Zarephath. There you will meet a widow. I have instructed her to feed you."

So Elijah went to Zarephath. At the gate to the town, he saw a woman gathering sticks. He asked her for some water and bread.

Olive oil was very important to the people in biblical times. It was made by pressing olives and was used for food, fuel, and even medicine.

She answered him, "I only have a small amount of flour in a jar and a little oil in a bottle, just enough to make one more meal for myself and my son."

"Don't worry," said Elijah. "Go ahead and make a meal for your son, but first make a small loaf of bread for me. God has promised that the flour and oil will not run out until this drought is over."

So she did as Elijah had said, and she always had enough flour in the jar and enough oil in the bottle to feed Elijah and her family— just as God had promised.

Growth Spurt

- What do you do when you need something?
- What did Elijah need?
- How did God help Elijah?

God provided everything that Elijah needed. There was always enough food to feed him and the widow's family. He will take care of your needs too!

Queen Esther
Esther 1-8

King Xerxes wanted a new wife. He had all the prettiest young girls in the country brought to the palace, so that he could choose the one that he liked best. Esther was one of these girls. She was very beautiful, and the king fell in love with her immediately. They were married, and she became Queen Esther.

The king did not know that Esther was Jewish. She was raised by her older cousin, Mordecai, and he had warned her not to tell the king.

Sprout says:
Have you ever stood up for someone?

87

One day as Mordecai was sitting at the entrance
to the palace, he heard two men plotting to kill
King Xerxes. He quickly went to tell Esther.
She told the king of the plan and saved his life.

Soon afterward, the king promoted a man
called Haman to be the highest leader in the
land, and everyone was ordered to bow down
to him. All of the servants in the palace bowed
to him, but Mordecai refused to bow to anyone
but God. This made Haman very angry. He was
angry at all of the Jewish people. So he went to
the king and said, "I think that we should get
rid of these Jewish people who are living in our
country. They are different from us." The king
agreed with him, and a decree was sent through-
out the land that all of the Jewish people would
be killed.

When Mordecai heard this, he tore his clothes
and wailed. Esther heard about Mordecai, so

she sent for him to ask him what was wrong. He told her that she should go and ask the king to change the decree and let the Jewish people live.

Esther was very frightened because the king might decide to kill her. But she asked Mordecai and all the other Jewish people to fast and pray for three days.

After three days she put on her best clothes and went to see the king. He was sitting on his throne, and when he saw her he was pleased. He held up his golden scepter and asked her what she wanted. "I'd like you and Haman to come to dinner," she said. After dinner she asked the king if he and Haman would come to dinner again.

The next day, while they were eating, the king asked her again, "What would you like me to do for you?"

This time Esther answered, "I want you to spare the lives of all my people. It has been ordered that we are all to be destroyed."

"Who has done this to you?" cried King Xerxes.

Esther pointed at Haman and said, "This is the evil man!" The king immediately had Haman arrested and made Mordecai a leader in his place.

Then he changed the decree so that the Jewish people would not be killed. The Jews were very happy and celebrated by feasting and giving gifts to each other.

- Has anyone ever stood up for you?

Queen Esther stood up for the Jewish people. God is pleased with us when we stand up for others.

The Blazing Furnace
Daniel 3

During the time when Nebuchadnezzar was king in Babylon, there were three young Jewish men serving in his kingdom. Their names were Shadrach, Meshach, and Abednego.

Now King Nebuchadnezzar built a huge gold statue— ninety feet high and nine feet wide. He placed it near Babylon and commanded that everyone should worship the golden statue. He said, "As soon as you hear the sound of a horn, flute, zither, lyre, harp, pipes, or any kind of music, you must bow down and worship the statue. If you do not, you will immediately be thrown into a blazing hot furnace!"

As soon as the people heard any kind of music, they would fall down and worship the statue made of gold.

There were some men who noticed that Shadrach, Meshach, and Abednego did not worship the statue, so they went and told the king.

The king was angry and had the three Jewish men brought to him. He asked them, "Is it true that you refuse to worship my golden statue? Don't you know that if you will not bow to it, I will have you thrown into the blazing fire? No one will be able to save you, not even a god. I will give you a second chance to worship the statue, but if you refuse again you are going into the roaring fire." Shadrach, Meshach, and Abednego replied, "We will not worship any other gods or the golden statue. We worship only the true God of Israel, and He will be able to rescue us if He chooses to do so." These words made the King furious, and he ordered the furnace to be heated seven times hotter than usual. Then he told the soldiers to bind up Shadrach, Meshach, and Abednego and throw them into the fire.

So the soldiers tied them up and took them to the furnace. It was so hot that the soldiers were killed by the flames. The three young men fell into the blazing fire.

Suddenly King Nebuchadnezzar jumped to his feet in amazement. "Didn't we throw three men into the furnace?" he asked his men. "We did," they answered. "Then why can I see FOUR men walking around in the fire?!" shouted the surprised king. He went near the opening of the furnace and called out, "Shadrach, Meshach, and Abednego, servants of the true God, come out of the fire!"

The three men came out of the fire, and everyone crowded around to look at them. They were amazed to see that nothing had happened to them. The fire had not burned them; not one hair on their heads was burnt, and they didn't even smell of smoke.

King Nebuchadnezzar said, "Praise the God of Shadrach, Meshach, and Abednego. They trusted Him to save them, and He sent His angel to help them. From this day on, no one is allowed to say anything bad about the three young Jewish men."

- Do you always stand up for what you believe?
- How did Shadrach, Meshach, and Abednego stand up for what they believed?
- How did God honor this?

Shadrach, Meshach, and Abednego stood up for what they believed by refusing to worship the golden statue. God honored them by sending an angel to protect them. He is happy when we only worship Him.

Daniel in the Lions' Den
Daniel 6

Nobody could beat Daniel. He was good! He was so good that when Darius took over as the king of Babylon he reorganized his kingdom and appointed Daniel as one of the leaders. Some of the other leaders were jealous and tried to find ways to make Daniel look bad, but Daniel had lived such a good life that they could not find anything to accuse him of. So they made another plan.

Sprout says:
What are you scared of?

99

They went to the king and said, "Oh King Darius, we think you should make a law that says no one will be allowed to pray to any god or man, except you, for the next thirty days. If they do, you will have them thrown into the lions' den." The king agreed to make this law.

As soon as Daniel heard about the new law, he went to his house. Upstairs in front of an open window, he knelt and prayed to God, just as he'd always done. The jealous leaders saw him praying and asking God for help. They went straight to King Darius.

"We saw Daniel praying to God," they said. "He must be thrown into the lions' den. That is the new law," they reminded the king.

King Darius was very upset, but he could do nothing to save Daniel. So he ordered them to put him into the lions' den. Then he said to Daniel, "I know that your God will look after you." A big block of stone was placed over the opening to the den, and the king went back to his palace. He was too sad to eat or sleep that night.

Early the next morning, the king hurried to the den. As he came near it he called out, "Daniel, Daniel, was your God able to save you from the lions?"

"Yes," Daniel answered. "God sent his angel to shut the mouths of the lions, so that they could not hurt me."

The king was very happy and ordered his men to lift Daniel out of the den. There wasn't a scratch on him because he had trusted God. The jealous leaders were thrown into the lions' den instead. Then the king made a new law that everyone must worship Daniel's God because He is the only true living God!

- Do you think that Daniel was scared of the lions?
- What did Daniel do when he was scared?
- How did God protect him from the lions?

God answered Daniel's prayers by sending an angel to shut the lions' mouths. He will answer your prayers, too!

Jonah and the Fish
Jonah 1-3

This is a story about a man who didn't catch a fish but was caught by a fish! His name was Jonah, and he was God's prophet. A prophet gives messages from God to His people.

One day God told Jonah to go to the city of Nineveh. The people who lived in that city were very wicked, and God wanted Jonah to tell them that He would punish them if they did not stop being bad. But Jonah did not want to go into Nineveh, so he decided to run as far from God as he could.

Sprout says:
Do you ever feel like running away?

Jonah went down to the harbor in Joppa and found a ship that was getting ready to sail to Tarshish. He paid for a ticket and went on board.

As they were sailing across the sea, God sent a big storm with strong winds. The boat was tossed around by the waves, and the sailors were terrified. "We are going to drown," they cried. "What are we going to do?" They threw everything into the sea to try to lighten the ship. All this time Jonah was sound asleep in the hold of the ship.

Did you know that nearly 71 percent of the earth is covered with water?

The captain of the ship went to Jonah. "Wake up and see what is happening to us," he shouted. "Ask your god to save us!"

Jonah knew that the storm was because of his disobedience. He told the captain that he was running away from God. The waves were getting bigger and bigger, and the ship was about to sink.

"What must we do to save ourselves?" the frightened sailors asked him.

"Pick me up and throw me into the sea," replied Jonah. So they threw him overboard, and immediately the wind stopped blowing and the sea became calm.

God sent a very large fish that swallowed Jonah, and for three days and three nights he was inside the smelly belly of the fish. He was really sorry that he had disobeyed God, so he prayed to God and said, "I am sorry that I didn't do what you asked. Please save me, and I will do what you want me to." Then God made the fish spit Jonah out onto the dry land.

Once again God asked Jonah to go to Nineveh and give them the message. This time Jonah was obedient

and went right away. When the people there heard that God was angry with them for being bad, they were sorry and stopped doing wicked things. God forgave them.

Growth Spurt

- Do you ever not want to do something?
- Can you run away from God?

Jonah disobeyed God and tried to run away, but God had a plan for him. Jonah learned that it's better to obey God the first time.

Mary, Jesus's Mother
Luke 1

The angel might as well have yelled surprise, he scared Mary so much. But he didn't. He said, "Good morning, Mary. God is very pleased with you and wants to bless you." Mary was a young girl who lived in Nazareth. She was engaged to be married to Joseph. The person who spoke to her was God's angel, Gabriel.

Mary was frightened when she saw the angel and wondered what he meant. But he assured her that she did not have to be afraid. "God has chosen you to give birth to a son. His name will be Jesus, and He will be God's very own Son. He will rule over the whole world."

Sprout says:
Have you ever been surprised?

Mary was shocked. "How can this be true?" she asked. "I don't understand!"

Gabriel answered, "Nothing's impossible for God. Don't worry; it will be the work of the Holy Spirit. Then your baby will be holy. He will be the Holy Son of God!" The angel also told her that her cousin Elizabeth would have a baby, even though she was quite old.

Mary replied, "I will do whatever God wants me to do." Then the angel left her.

Mary was so excited that she hurried to visit Elizabeth. Mary was very happy and could not wait to tell her the good news. She sang a song of praise to God because He had chosen to bless her. Mary stayed with Elizabeth for three months, and then she returned home.

Growth Spurt

- Do you think Mary was surprised by the angel's visit?
- What did the angel tell Mary?

The angel Gabriel surprised Mary by telling her that God would bless her with a son named Jesus. It was all part of God's plan to send His Son to earth.

The Birth of Jesus
Luke 2

Caesar Augustus gave an order that a census must be taken. Each person had to return to their hometown to be counted.

Joseph's family was from the town of Bethlehem, so he and Mary traveled there to be registered. When they arrived they could not find a place to stay, and the time came for the baby to be born. Mary wrapped little Jesus in cloths and placed Him in a manger.

Sprout says:
Do you like to give gifts?

That night in the fields nearby, shepherds were
looking after their sheep. Suddenly an angel of
the Lord appeared before them. He shone with
the light of God's glory, and they were terrified.

But the angel said, "Don't be afraid. I am here to bring you good news! Today the Savior of the world was born. He is Christ the Lord. Go and find the baby who is wrapped in cloths and lying in a manger."

At once the whole sky was filled with thousands of angels singing praises to God. When the angels were gone, the shepherds hurried into Bethlehem and found Joseph and Mary with the baby lying in a manger. When they saw the baby, they believed everything the angels had said was true. They told everyone about the baby and what the angels had said about Him. The people were amazed when they heard the shepherds' story. But Mary was quiet and kept her thoughts to herself.

The shepherds returned, and they celebrated by praising and glorifying God for all the things they'd seen and heard.

Did you know Jesus's Hebrew name was Jeshua, which means "the Lord is Salvation?" In Greek it is pronounced Jesus.

Growth Spurt

- How do you feel when you receive a gift?
- What gift did God give us?
- When do we celebrate this gift?

On Christmas we celebrate the birth of Jesus Christ. He is God's amazing gift to everyone.

The Wise Men
Matthew 2

Where is the baby? Lots of people were asking the question—some for good reasons and some for evil reasons.

During the reign of King Herod, some wise men from the east traveled to Jerusalem. They asked around, "Where is the newborn child who will become king of the Jews? We saw his star in the east and have come to worship him."

Sprout says:
Do you like to visit friends?

121

When King Herod heard this, he was very upset and quickly called his chief priests and teachers of the law. "Where is this baby supposed to be born?" he asked them.

"In Bethlehem," they replied.

So Herod called the wise men and told them to go and find the child and to let him know where he is. As soon as the wise men heard what the king had to say, they left and followed the star until it stopped over a house. They were very happy to see Mary and the baby Jesus. They bowed down and worshiped Him. They gave Him gifts of gold, frankincense, and myrrh. Then they left, but they did not return to tell Herod where the baby was because they had been warned in a dream not to return.

Frankincense and myrrh were precious treasures from the East. They were used for perfume, medicine, and in many rituals.

After the wise men were gone, Joseph had a dream. The angel of God came to tell him, "Get up, take Mary and the baby Jesus, and escape to Egypt. Stay there because King Herod wants to kill the baby." Joseph took Mary and Jesus and fled to Egypt that night. Herod was

The Roman army was like the police during Jesus's time. There were over 6,000 foot soldiers alone!

123

very angry when he heard that the wise men had not obeyed him. He didn't know where Jesus was, so he ordered his soldiers to kill all the little boys in Bethlehem.

Much later, after Herod was dead, the angel of God came to Joseph once again and told him that it was safe to return to Israel. So Joseph went back to Israel with Mary and Jesus. They went to live in a town called Nazareth.

- Who went to visit the baby Jesus?
- What did they bring Him?
- What was the warning they were given?

God used an angel to warn Mary and Joseph about Herod's evil plan. They escaped to safety in Egypt. God protected them, and He will protect you.

John the Baptist
Matthew 3, John 1

Not many people eat bugs, but John did. He ate locusts and wild honey. He wore rough clothes made from camel's hair with a leather belt around his waist. People came from Jerusalem, Judea, and all over Jordan to see him and listen to what he had to say. The people called him John the Baptist because he told them they should change the way they lived and be baptized.

Among the crowds were many of the leaders in the church. When John saw that they also wanted to

Sprout says:
Who is your favorite teacher?

be baptized because everyone else was doing it, he got angry and shouted at them, "What do you think you are doing? Do you think that just by being baptized you are going to change your lives? No! You must also confess your sins, and then your life will change."

John also told them, "Someone else is coming after me who is so powerful that I am not even worthy to carry His sandals. He will change your lives by baptizing you with the Holy Spirit."

Then Jesus came from Galilee to the Jordan River to be baptized by John. When John saw Him standing on the bank of the river, he said, "Look, here is the Lamb of God. He will take away the sins of the world." At first John did not want to baptize Jesus and said, "I am the one who needs to be baptized by you."

Did you know that in every beehive there is a queen bee with about 200 drone bees and 20,000 to 80,000 worker bees?

But Jesus insisted, "This is the way God wants it to be done."

So John agreed to baptize Jesus. As soon as Jesus stood up out of the water, the skies opened and He saw the Spirit of God coming down. It looked like a dove that flew down and landed on Him. A voice from heaven said, "This is my Son. I love Him with all of my heart, and I am very pleased with Him!"

Did you know that the Jordan River flows all the way from the Sea of Galilee to the Dead Sea? It is mentioned around 200 times in the Bible, including four times when God parts the water.

Growth Spurt

- What did John the Baptist teach the people?
- Why did John baptize Jesus?
- What happened when Jesus was baptized?

God was pleased when John baptized Jesus. He used this to show the people that Jesus was His Son and that He loved Him very much.

The Paralyzed Man
Luke 5

One day a large crowd gathered to listen to Jesus teaching. Among them were many Pharisees and religious teachers. Jesus was filled with the power of God and was able to heal the sick people who came to Him for help.

Some men arrived carrying their friend on a mat. He was paralyzed and could not walk. They tried to take him into the house to see Jesus, but it was too crowded for them to even get through the door.

Sprout says:
Have you ever been hurt?

133

At that time the houses had flat roofs. The people used them for doing chores like weaving and spinning wool. During the hot summers, they would also sleep on the roofs so that they could be out in the fresh air.

The friends had to make another plan. They knew that Jesus would be able to help them if they could only get inside the house. So they carried the paralyzed man up onto the roof and made a hole by removing some of the roof tiles. Then they carefully lowered him through the opening until he was right in the middle of the room in front of Jesus. The men begged Jesus to heal their friend so that he could walk again. Jesus saw the paralyzed man and his friends truly believed that he could be healed. He said, "Friend, your sins are forgiven."

The Pharisees and the religious leaders heard what Jesus said and began thinking to themselves,
"Who does he think he is?
Does he think he is God?
Only God can forgive sins!"

Jesus knew exactly what they were thinking, and He said, "Which is easier: to say, 'I forgive your sins' or 'Get up and walk?' I want you to know that I am truly God's Son, and to prove it to you I am going to do both." Then He spoke to the paralyzed man, "Get up, take your mat and go home!" Immediately the man stood up, took the mat he'd been lying on, and went home praising God.

Everyone in the house was overwhelmed by what they'd seen. They could hardly believe their eyes! Awestruck, they began to praise God by saying, "We have never seen anything like that! Today we saw an amazing miracle!"

Growth Spurt

- How did the paralyzed man's friends help him?
- What did Jesus do to help him?

Jesus healed the paralyzed man because of his friends' faithfulness. God will honor your faithfulness when you believe in Him.

Jesus's Disciples
Matthew 4-10

C ome with me, and I will show you how to catch people instead of fish," Jesus said to two brothers who were fishermen. Simon Peter and Andrew immediately dropped their nets and went with Jesus.

A little way further along the shore of the Sea of Galilee, Jesus saw two more brothers, James and John. They were sitting in a boat with their father, Zebedee,

Sprout says:
Have you ever gone fishing?

preparing their fishing nets. Once again Jesus said, "Follow me." They left their boat and their father and followed Him at once.

They traveled with Jesus all over Galilee teaching people about the kingdom of God and healing those who were sick.

Some time later Jesus saw a man named Matthew who was sitting in a tax collector's booth taking taxes from the people. Jesus went to him and said, "Come along with me." Matthew got up and followed Him.

Jesus called twelve of His followers and told them that they were to go out and help people by making them well again. These are the names of those He sent out: Simon Peter, Andrew, James, John, Philip, Bartholomew, Thomas, Matthew, James, Thaddeus, Simon, and Judas, the one who would later betray Him.

To them He said, "Go and find those people who are lost or sick and help them. I am giving you the power to make people well and to raise them from the dead. Teach everyone about the kingdom of God."

After Jesus had given these instructions to His followers, He preached and taught all over Galilee.

Growth Spurt

- What were Peter and Andrew doing?
- What did Jesus tell them to fish for instead?
- How did Jesus want them to fish for people?

God wants us to help people just as the disciples did.

Jesus Teaches the People
Matthew 5-6

What's going on?" "What's He saying?"
"Let me through; I can't see." A large crowd
of people had gathered to listen to Jesus.
Everyone wanted to hear what He was saying.
So Jesus walked a little way up the mountain-
side and sat down to teach them. He spoke
about many things—things that would help
them to live as God wanted them to. He told
people that they were to be like lamps that
shine in the darkness. If they let their lights
shine, then other people will come to know
God and to worship Him.

He also said, "It is easy to love your friends,
but it is just as important to love those people
who are not always good to you. Pray for
them—this is what God wants you to do."

Then He taught them how to pray. "Don't think that you need to speak to God in a loud voice and with many big words; this will only impress people," Jesus said. "Rather find a quiet place and simply tell God what you want. He will listen to you. He knows what you need because He loves you. All you need to say is:

Our Father in heaven, Your name is holy and honored. Let your kingdom come soon. Let Your will be done here on earth, as it is in heaven. Give us food for today and forgive us when we sin, as we forgive others who sin against us. Keep us from temptation and the devil. For everything belongs to You, and You are powerful and glorious. Amen."

Growth Spurt

- Do you pray to God?
- What did Jesus teach the people?
- Is God happy when we pray to Him?

Jesus taught the people that it is important to pray every day. When we pray we thank God for what He's given us and ask Him for what we need. God is happy when we pray!

Jesus Calms the Storm
Mark 4

A mighty storm attacked the boat that Jesus was sleeping in. He and his disciples were crossing the lake, and the little boat was being tossed about on the waves. The wind was blowing, and the waves were crashing into the boat, filling it with water. The disciples were terrified. "We are going to drown!" they cried. "Wake up!" they shouted to Jesus. "The boat is sinking, and we are going to die! Don't you even care if we die?"

Sprout says:
Have you ever been in a storm?

Jesus stood up and said to the wind and the waves, "Silence! Calm down!"

Immediately the wind stopped blowing and the sea became as smooth as glass. Then He said to the disciples, "Why are you so afraid? Don't you have any faith at all?"

The disciples were awestruck and whispered to one another, "What kind of a man is this? Who is He? Even the wind and the waves obey Him!"

Growth Spurt

- Have you ever been scared in a storm?
- What did the disciples do when they were scared?
- What did Jesus do to help them?

God is so powerful that
He can do anything.
He will look after you!

Jesus and the Children
Luke 18

"Go away!" the men told the children. People were always coming to Jesus to be healed. He made the sick people well, the lame people walk, the deaf people hear, and those who were blind see again. Crowds of people always surrounded Jesus, and they often brought their little children to Him, hoping that He would touch them and bless them.

When the disciples saw this, they tried to chase the children away.

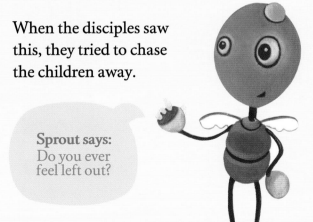

Sprout says:
Do you ever feel left out?

"Don't bother Jesus," they said. "He is too busy to help you."

Jesus heard what they said, and He was angry with them. He scolded them saying, "Don't push these children away. Never come between them and me. Remember this: they belong in God's kingdom— and unless you accept God's kingdom like a little child does, you will never enter it."

Then He called the children to Him, picked them up in His arms, and blessed them.

Growth Spurt

- How do you feel when you're left out?
- What did Jesus tell the disciples?
- Does Jesus have time for you?

Jesus told the children to come to Him so that He could bless them. He always has time for you!

156

Loaves and Fishes
Mark 6, John 6

J esus is leaving! He's going to the other side
of the lake!" the people shouted to each other.
And they were right. The disciples had been
with Jesus telling Him about all the things they
had done and taught, when He said to them,
"Let's go away and take a little break, so that
we can get some rest." They got into a boat and
sailed across the Sea of Galilee to a quiet place.

Sprout says:
Have you ever
been hungry?

Soon people were running from all the surrounding towns to meet them. When Jesus arrived on the other shore, He saw the large crowd of people and immediately felt compassion for them. So He started teaching them and healing those who were sick.

By now it was getting late, so the disciples came to Jesus and said, "It is late and we are far from town. Send the people away so they can go and find something to eat."

But He answered them, "You give them something to eat."

Bread was made
by grinding barley
between two stones.
On special occasions
mint or cinnamon was
added for flavor.

The disciples were shocked. "We don't have enough money to buy food for so many people," they replied.

"How many loaves do you have?" asked Jesus.

They quickly went to see what they could find, but when they returned all they had found was one little boy who had only five small loaves and two fish.

Jesus told them to make everyone sit down on the green grass, in groups of hundreds and fifties. Then He took the five loaves and two fish, looked up to heaven, and said a prayer of thanks.

Next He broke the loaves and gave them to the disciples to hand out to the people. He also divided the two small fish among them all. Everyone ate until they were full. Then the disciples picked up the leftover pieces. They filled twelve baskets with broken pieces of fish and bread.

It was amazing—more than 5,000 people had been fed!

Growth Spurt

- What did the disciples do when the people were hungry?
- What did Jesus do to feed the people?
- Was there enough food for everyone?

Jesus fed 5,000 people with only two fish and five small loaves of bread. He will provide for you, too.

Jesus Meets Zaccaeus
Luke 18-19

J esus!" someone yelled. "JESUS!" Jesus and
the disciples were on their way to Jerusalem,
and they had just arrived outside the city walls of
Jericho. Who was calling to Him? It was a blind
man who begged Jesus for help. Jesus could see that
the man really believed he would be healed, so He
said to the man, "Receive your sight." Immediately
the man could see again! He was so excited that he
followed Jesus shouting praises to God.

Sprout says:
Have you ever
taken something
that wasn't yours?

When the people heard what had happened, they gathered around Jesus. The large crowd followed Him all the way into the city of Jericho.

Now in that city there lived a man whose name was Zacchaeus. He was the chief tax collector and quite a rich man. He wanted to see who Jesus was and what was going on, but he was too short. He could not see over the heads of all the people in front of him. So he ran ahead of Jesus down the road and climbed up into a sycamore-fig tree.

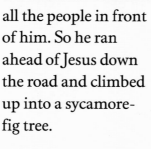

He was hoping to see Jesus as He walked by.

When Jesus got to the tree, He stopped, looked up, and said, "Zacchaeus, come down now. I want to visit your house today." Zacchaeus could hardly believe his ears! Jesus was coming to his house! So he scrambled down from the tree, happy to be able to take Jesus home with him.

All the people standing around heard what was going on, and they began to complain, "Why does Jesus want to be friends with such a crook?" they muttered. But Zacchaeus said to Jesus, "I will give away half of what I own to the poor people, and if I've cheated anyone, I will pay them back four times what I took from them."

Jesus was very pleased and said to Zacchaeus, "Today you will be saved. I came to find those who are lost and to save them."

- Has anyone ever taken something that is yours?
- What did Zacchaeus take from the people?
- How did he make up for it?

When Zacchaeus met Jesus, he realized that it was wrong to steal money from people. He did the right thing by paying everyone back. God is happy when we're honest too.

168

Jesus and the Cross
Matthew 26-27

Jesus was really sad. Why was He so troubled? He and His disciples finished eating the Passover dinner, and they went to the Mount of Olives and into the Garden of Gethsemane. What was wrong? Jesus was very sad because He knew the time had come for Him to die. The reason God had sent Him to earth was so that He could die for the sins of all people.

He went away by Himself to pray. When Jesus returned He found the disciples fast asleep. "Wake up," He said. "The time has come for me to be betrayed. Get up, let's go."

Sprout says:
Have you ever let a friend down?

169

He was still speaking when Judas, who was one of the disciples, arrived. Judas had a large crowd of people with him, including soldiers carrying swords and clubs. Judas went to Jesus and kissed Him saying, "How are you, Rabbi?"

Jesus knew that this kiss was a sign to the soldiers, and He said, "Friend, do what you came to do." Jesus knew that Judas had betrayed Him for thirty silver coins. The soldiers stepped forward, grabbed Jesus, and arrested Him. Then they took Him to the Chief Priest, who decided that Jesus should die. Meanwhile, the other disciples ran away as quickly as they could because they were afraid.

Early the next morning, Jesus was taken to the governor, Pilate, by the chief priests and the elders. They demanded that He be nailed to a cross. Pilate could see that Jesus was innocent, but the people were shouting for Jesus to die. Pilate tried to persuade them to kill Barabbas, who was a very bad man, instead of Jesus, but the crowd would not listen to him. When Pilate saw that the crowd was starting to get out of hand, he set Barabbas free and gave Jesus to them saying, "Do what you want with Him."

Then the soldiers led Jesus away. They whipped Him, put a crown of thorns on His head and forced Him to carry a cross to a hill, called Golgotha, outside the city. There they nailed Him to the cross and put a sign on the cross that said: "THIS IS JESUS, THE KING OF THE JEWS." They also crucified two robbers, one on Jesus's left and one on His right.

Did you know that Judas was paid thirty pieces of silver for betraying Jesus? Each piece was equal to four days' wages.

In the middle of the day, the whole earth became dark. Jesus called out to God for the last time and died. At that moment a huge earthquake shook the ground and the buildings, and the curtain in the temple was torn from top to bottom. The soldiers who were guarding Jesus were terrified and said to one another, "This has to be the Son of God!"

Late in the afternoon, a rich man named Joseph of Arimathea went to Pilate and asked for Jesus's body. Pilate gave it to him, so Joseph took Jesus's body and wrapped it in clean linens. Then he placed Him in a new tomb and rolled a very large stone in front of the entrance. Pilate ordered soldiers to guard the tomb so that no one could get into it.

Growth Spurt

- What did Judas do to Jesus in the Garden of Gethsemane?
- What did the soldiers do to Him?
- What did they realize after He died?

Jesus really was the Son of God. He came to earth to die on the cross for all of our sins.

173

Easter Morning
Luke 24

Very early in the morning on the Sunday after Jesus's death, some of the women who loved Him went to His tomb. They brought spices with them to anoint His body. But when they arrived, they were shocked to find that the stone had been rolled away and the tomb was open. They walked right in and did not find the body of Jesus as they had expected. Instead, they saw two men dressed in shining white clothes. The women were terrified!

Sprout says:
Why do we celebrate Easter?

The men said to them, "I know you are looking for Jesus. He is no longer here. He is alive! He has risen! Remember He told you that He would die, but after three days He would rise again?" Then the women remembered that Jesus had said this. So they ran back to tell the others.

During Jesus's time the Jewish people wrapped the bodies of dead people from head to toe with sheets of linen. They also sprinkled them with fragrant spices.

The disciples did not believe what the women were saying. So Peter ran to the tomb to see for himself. When he got there, he looked inside and saw only the strips of cloth lying there. He wondered what had happened to Jesus.

A little while later, two of Jesus's friends were walking along the road to the village of Emmaus. Suddenly Jesus came up and walked with them. He told them many things about Himself. They hurried back to tell the other disciples what had happened. "We have seen Jesus!" they said, but no one believed them.

While they were still talking about all that had happened in the past three days, Jesus appeared in the room. "Peace to you," He said. They were very frightened because they thought He was a ghost. But He said to them, "Don't be upset. See, it is really I. Come on, touch me." And He showed them His hands and feet. They were filled with joy and amazement. Jesus asked them for something to eat, and they gave Him a piece of fish.

After that Jesus spent some time with the disciples. He taught them how to read and understand the Bible, so that they would be able to teach other people about God's plan of salvation for everyone. He also told them they should stay in Jerusalem and wait for God to send them His power from Heaven. Then the disciples could go out to the whole world and tell people about everything they had seen and heard.

Growth Spurt

- What did the women find in the tomb?
- Where was Jesus?
- What did He tell the disciples?

Just as God had promised, Jesus rose from the dead after three days. We celebrate Easter to remember this amazing promise.

Jesus's Gift to His Followers

Acts 2

Swoosh! Everyone was startled by the sound of a strong wind filling the whole house. It was the day of Pentecost, after Jesus left them to go to heaven, and His followers were meeting together. No one knew where the sound came from. They saw flames that looked like fire above each person's head. All of them were filled with the Holy Spirit and began speaking in different languages.

Sprout says:
Do you know any other languages?

At that time there were many Jews from all over the world staying in Jerusalem. When they heard the sound, they came running to see what was going on. To their amazement they heard the friends of Jesus all speaking in different languages. Everyone was able to understand what the disciples were saying, because they heard them telling about the wonders of God in their own languages. They were astounded and confused!

Some people thought they had been drinking too much wine and made fun of them. But Peter stood up, along with the other disciples, and said in a loud voice,

Did you know that Pentecost is also called the Feast of Weeks, and it celebrated the end of the grain harvest?

"My fellow Jews and all of you who live in Jerusalem, listen carefully. These people are not drunk. What you are seeing today is what the prophet Joel told us would happen. You saw Jesus doing so many miracles and wonderful things that you knew He came from God, but still you gave Him up to be nailed to a cross to die. God has raised Him from the dead! He is now in heaven and has sent the Holy Spirit to help us. That is what you see happening here today."

During Pentecost Pilgrims traveled to Jerusalem from all over Palestine and the Roman Empire to take part in the ceremonies and celebrate.

When the people heard this, they were very upset and asked, "What must we do now?"

Peter answered them, "Turn away from your sins, ask God to forgive you, and be baptized in the name of Jesus. Then you will also receive the Holy Spirit as God promised."

That day about 3,000 people listened to what Peter was saying and were baptized. They started praying, praising God, and telling others about Him. Every day more and more people believed in God and were saved.

- What happened to the disciples on the day of Pentecost?
- What did the people do when they heard God's message?

God helped the disciples speak in different languages so that the people could hear about Him. You can tell others about Him too!

The Road to Damascus
Acts 9

I'll kill them all!" That's what a man named Saul said about the followers of Jesus. He didn't like it that so many people were following Jesus. None of the religious leaders liked it. They started beating the Christians and putting them in jail. So the Christians were forced to leave their homes and go to other towns. Wherever they went they told people about Jesus and how to be saved.

Saul went to the high priest in Jerusalem and asked for permission to arrest all the Christians that he could find in the city of Damascus.

Sprout says:
Have you ever been on a trip?

As soon as he got the letters of permission, he set off to hunt them down.

As he got near to Damascus, a bright light suddenly flashed from heaven, and Saul fell on the ground. He heard a voice from heaven saying, "Saul, Saul, why are you trying to hurt me?" The men traveling with Saul were speechless. They could hear the sound, but they saw nothing.

"Who are you?" asked Saul.

"I am Jesus, the one you are trying to hurt," was the reply. "Now get up and go into the city. Wait there until you are told what to do." When Saul got up from the ground and opened his eyes, he couldn't see at all. So his friends took him by the hand and led him into the city. For three days he was blind and did not eat or drink a thing.

At that time there was a man called Ananias
living in Damascus. He was a disciple of Jesus.
God spoke to him saying, "Go to the house of
Judas on Straight Street and ask for a man named
Saul. You will find him there praying." Ananias
was afraid to go because he'd heard of the terrible
things that Saul was doing to the Christians.

But God told him to go anyway. "I have picked Saul to be my messenger to all the Gentiles, kings, and Jews," He said. So Ananias went.

He found Saul in the house and put his hands on Saul's eyes saying, "Jesus has sent me so that you will be able to see again and be filled with the Holy Spirit." Immediately something like scales fell off Saul's eyes and he could see again! He got up, was baptized, and had a meal with them.

After a few days Saul, later called Paul, began teaching that Jesus was the Son of God. Everyone was surprised to see how much Saul had changed.

Growth Spurt

- Why was Saul going to Damascus?
- What happened to him along the way?
- How did Saul change?

Even though Saul was bad,
God could change him.
He can help you change too!

Paul and Silas in Jail
Acts 16

On a day of worship, Paul and his friend Silas went down to the river to pray. They met a woman there named Lydia and told her about Jesus. She listened carefully to them, and God opened her heart so that she would believe in Him. After she and her family were baptized, she invited Paul and Silas to stay in her house.

One day as they were on their way to the river to pray, they met a young slave girl. Her owners used her to make money by telling people's fortunes.

Sprout says:
Do you always do what is right?

She was able to do this because of the evil spirit that was in her. She began shouting at Paul and Silas and would not stop. Finally Paul said, "In the name of Jesus, come out of her." The spirit left her, and she was calm. But now she could no longer tell fortunes. Her owners were very angry, and they grabbed Paul and Silas and took them to the judge. The judge ordered them to be beaten and thrown into jail. He also told the jailer to guard them very carefully.

They were put in a cell with their feet locked in stocks. Around midnight, Paul and Silas were praying and singing hymns to God. The other prisoners were listening to them. Suddenly, without warning, a violent earthquake shook the prison walls and all the doors flew open. Everyone's chains fell off, and they were set free!

The jailer woke up and came running to see what was going on. When he saw that all the prisoners were free, he wanted to kill himself. But Paul stopped him saying,
"Don't do that!
We are all here!
Nobody has run away!"

The poor jailer was so relieved that he collapsed on the ground in front of them asking, "What must I do to be saved?"

They replied, "Believe in the Lord Jesus, and you will be saved." The jailer took Paul and Silas to his home, and Paul explained the truth about Jesus to the jailer and his whole family. After hearing everything about Jesus, the whole family wanted to be baptized immediately. The jailer bandaged up the wounds of Paul and Silas, and together they enjoyed a meal. Everyone was very happy because now they trusted Jesus to save them. They had a big celebration!

The next morning the judge ordered the jailer to release Paul and Silas. They went back to Lydia's house to see their friends again.

Growth Spurt

- Why were Paul and Silas thrown into jail?
- What did they do in jail?
- What happened when they prayed?

Paul and Silas ended up in jail for doing the right thing. God honored this by setting them free. He will honor you when you do the right thing too!

John Tells of Jesus's Return
Revelation

A voice like a trumpet blasted in John's ear. John, one of Jesus's favorite disciples, was living in exile on the island of Patmos. One Sunday, while he was praying, a voice said to him, "Write on a scroll all that you see and send it to the seven churches in Ephesus, Smyrna, Pergamum, Thyatira, Sardis, Philadelphia, and Laodicea.

When John turned around to see who was speaking, he saw seven golden lamp stands. Jesus was

Sprout says:
Do you believe in Jesus?

standing there, wearing a long robe with a golden belt around His waist. His hair was as white as snow, and His eyes shone like fire. In His right hand, He held seven stars. John got such a fright that he fell down as if he were dead. Jesus placed His right hand on him and said, "Don't be afraid. I am the first and last. I was dead, but now I am alive forever. I am going to show you many wonderful things."

When John looked up, he saw a door that opened into heaven. He heard a voice saying,

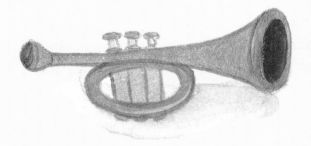

"Come in and I will show you what is going to happen in the future." He went up to heaven and saw someone sitting on a shining throne surrounded by thousands of angels. Next to the throne stood the Lamb of God, and everyone was singing songs of worship to Him.

An angel showed John how God was going to destroy the earth and all that was in it. Then the angel took John to see the new heaven and a new earth that God would create. It was BEAUTIFUL! The Holy City of Jerusalem had walls that sparkled like glass, decorated with precious jewels such as sapphires, emeralds, and amethysts. Each of the twelve gates was made out of a huge pearl, and the streets were pure gold. A beautiful river surrounded by fruit trees ran through the middle of the city, and at the center stood the throne of God and the Lamb. This is where God will live forever. In heaven there will be no more darkness, sickness, or crying. God will make everything new again!

The angel told John, "Everything that you have seen is true. Soon the Lord Jesus will return to earth to take those who believe in Him to live in heaven forever."

Growth Spurt

- What did Jesus show John in his dream?
- What will happen if we believe in Jesus?

God promises us
that heaven will
be amazing. If
you believe in
Him, you will
live forever
in heaven!

About the Authors and Illustrators

Robbie de Villiers is a graphic designer whose work has earned international recognition, including two Clio Awards for excellence in advertising and nineteen International Clio nominations. Robbie has created the Seedling and Sprout series with his wife, Dianne; his daughter, Michelle de Villiers-Newton; and his son, P.J. Originally from South Africa, the de Villiers family now lives in Connecticut.

For more fun, visit the Seedling and Sprout Web site at:

www.seedlingandsprout.com

Now available!
Sprout Storybooks

PURPLE SPOT SICKNESS

THE LONG SHORTCUT

Look out for the
Seedling Bible &
Storybooks!